The Buffets of Carnival

Carnival.

Entertaining Secrets from Carnival Chefs

Bountiful Buffets!

Dear Guests,

Your marvelous response to our first book, *Carnival Creations*, which featured mouth-watering recipes from Carnival chefs, was very gratifying. In fact, it was this rewarding experience that inspired *The Buffets of Carnival*, a culinary tour through the world-famous buffets that have delighted and awed thousands of guests on Carnival Cruise Lines.

This new book features a fascinating array of garnishing and decorating techniques, from seasonal fruit and vegetable presentations to intricately designed ice sculptures. Our Recipes for Entertaining section is an international tribute to succulent tastes and dazzling colors around the world, from Italy to California, from the sun-drenched shores of Greece to the mysterious Far East.

Of course, no book on the Buffets of Carnival would be complete without a look at the crown jewel of our dining experience – Carnival's Grand Gala Buffet, a sumptuous food extravaganza. Let us warn you – after you have read *The Buffets of Carnival*, you will never view dinner parties the same way again.

Join us at Carnival, the world's most popular cruise line, in a journey through a world of magical taste and beauty that only the unparalleled talents of the Carnival chefs could create. Welcome to the Buffets of Carnival.

Natko Nincevic
Vice President & General Manager
Seachest/Carnival Cruise Lines

FIRST EDITION. Copyright ©1998 Carnival Corporation. All rights reserved.
Carnival Place, 3655 N.W. 87 Avenue, Miami, Florida 33178-2428
Executive Offices: (305) 599-2600
www.carnival.com

"Carnival," the Reverse-C Logo, "The Most Popular Cruise Line in the World!" and "The Fun Ships"
are the registered service marks of Carnival Corporation

Book Design and Production by Tad Ware & Company, Inc.
Photographed at sea aboard the *Carnival Destiny* by Tad Ware Photography

Contents

The Carnival Experience
Page 4

Food Sculpture
Page 8

Ice Carving
Page 28

Carnival Buffets
Page 38

Volume Recipes
Page 50

Recipes for Entertaining
Page 58

Index
Page 86

The Carnival Experience

Food, fun and fantastic times make Carnival "The Most Popular Cruise Line in the World!®"

Courtesy of Carnival Cruise Lines

How It All Began

Carnival's quarter-century of cruising fun and elegance began with one ship and a simple strategy – provide our customers with a shipboard experience they would never forget.

Based in Miami, Florida, the Carnival Cruise Lines story opened with the ship *Mardi Gras* in 1972. Carnival soon developed our unique "Fun Ship"® concept, offering cruises so vibrant, with so many exciting, unusual activities that they appealed to people of virtually every age and background. The response from the public was phenomenal.

New ships soon followed, and Carnival assumed its position as "The Most Popular Cruise Line in the World!"® Today, more guests go home with happy memories of their time on Carnival than on any other cruise line.

As the public enthusiastically embraced "The Fun Ships"® experience, Carnival secured its position as industry leader with a series of new superliners. In fact, with the purchase of the *Destiny*, Carnival entered *The Guinness Book of Records*.

Courtesy of Carnival Cruise Lines

Constructed in Italy, the *Destiny* is the world's largest cruise ship, at over 101,000 gross registered tons.

Carnival continues its position of predominance with the introduction of two new superliners, the *Elation* and the *Paradise*, and the launching of another ship as large as the *Destiny* before the year 2000.

The Carnival Buffet

As in every element of the cruise experience, Carnival is committed to providing its guests with a unique, unforgettable dining experience. We have found that guests like things elegant, yet easy – a wide variety of food, exquisitely presented, available in a relaxed, convenient format. The answer has been the Buffets of Carnival – a feast of globally-inspired culinary delights, sprinkled with the elegance, fun and magic that our guests have come to expect from Carnival Cruise Lines.

Courtesy of Carnival Cruise Lines

As you step up to one of our buffets, you enter a special world created by the Carnival chefs – a land of temptation and delight where you wander amazed from enticing platters of Italian risotto and warm foccacia to inviting casseroles of savory eggplant moussaka. Appetizers, salads, entrées, desserts – each dish reflects the Carnival chefs'

Courtesy of Carnival Cruise Lines

remarkable talent and painstaking attention, delighting the eye as extravagantly as it does the palate. And every night this gastronomic wonderland is transformed, with a new theme, fantastic presentations, and unique dining creations.

We hope that the recipes and techniques on the following pages will spark special memories and inspire you to create your own buffet magic in the proud Carnival tradition.

Courtesy of Carnival Cruise Lines

Did You Know...

During the course of a 7-day cruise, our guests will consume the following:

Prime Rib . . . . . . 1400 lb	Hamburgers . . . . . 9000 ea	Pasta . . . . 2300 lb	Apples . . . . . . 3500 ea
Chicken . . . . 3000 lb	Hot Dogs . . . . 600 lb	Tomatoes . . . . 4000 lb	Pineapples . . . . 1560 ea
Duck . . . . 600 lb	Ham . . . . 1200 lb	Heads of Lettuce . . 4000 ea	Potatoes . . . . . 8000 lb
Shrimp . . . . 3000 lb	Salmon . . . . 600 lb	Cucumbers . . . . . . 1100 lb	Bell Peppers . . . . 1800 lb
Veal . . . . 800 lb	Smoked Salmon . . . 400 lb	Bananas . . . . 6320 ea	

Breakfast lovers will enjoy:

Eggs 42,000	Coffee . . . . . . 1800 lb	Bagels . . . . 1160 ea	Indv. Cereals . . . 6200 boxes
Slices of Bacon 45,000	Fruit Juice . . . . . . 920 gal	Butter . . . . 1400 lb	
Link Sausage . . . . . . 600 lb	Milk . . . . 110 gal	Grits . . . . 90 lb	

Pastries made on board will include the following ingredients:

Cake Mix . . . . 1970 lb	Flour . . . . 8200 lb	Shortening . . . . 1620 lb

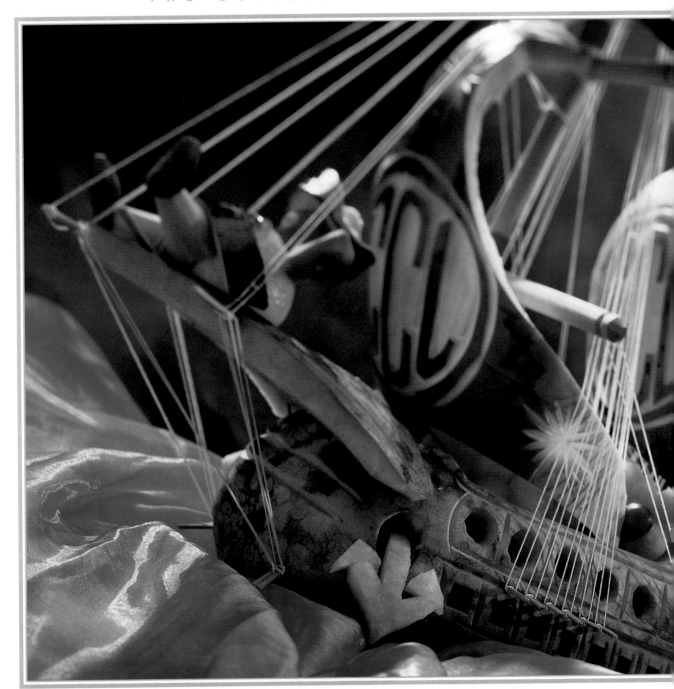

Food Sculpture

The secrets of fantastic presentation that transform
Carnival's gourmet foods into a feast for
both the eyes and the palate.

Easy Garnishes

Tomato Rose

STEP 1

Select a tomato that is at room temperature. Starting at its top, peel along its circumference, creating one long, thin strip of tomato skin approximately one inch wide. (Slide the paring knife back and forth slowly, and peel the skin shallow enough so that the seeds are not exposed.) Do not detach the end of the peel from the tomato.

STEP 2

Leave a circle at the base of the tomato approximately two inches in diameter and one-half inch thick unpeeled, to serve as the rose base.

STEP 3

With the tomato base in one hand and the attached peel in the other, wrap the peel around the base as shown in the illustration. The longer the peel you have created, the more attractive rose you can make.

Flock of Birds

Yellow Squash Bird

STEP 1

Cut away an area approximately one-half inch thick and three inches long at a slant from the sides of a yellow squash. This will be the bird's tail. On another squash, perform the same cuts on an area approximately one inch thick and five inches long. This will be the wing.

STEP 2

Hold the wings together, with the outer skins facing each other and the pointed areas to the top. Shape the wings as shown in the illustration. Cut a cavity at the end of the squash, and attach the tail with a toothpick. Attach the wings on both concave sides of the squash.

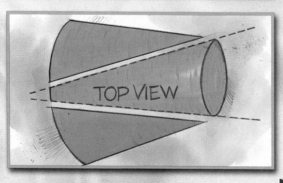

TOP VIEW

STEP 3

To create the bill, cut off two inches from a carrot that is approximately one inch wide. Trim one end by following the carrot's circumference, leaving one end smaller than the other. Make a slanted cut on both sides, as shown by the dotted lines in the illustration. Cut a V-shape on the wider portion, and attach it to the bird with toothpicks.

Watermelon Seahorse

STEP 1

Cut off the end of a melon. Scrape away the skin from its front, and use a pencil to draw a seahorse on the exposed area. Use your knife to cut along the dotted line marked "A", cutting straight one inch deep and then sliding the knife down. Do the same along the "B" line, but slant the cut to meet the first cut and make a cavity around the shaded area.

STEP 2

Trim the areas marked "A" to elevate the nose and tail. Trim the areas marked "B" to elevate the seaweeds. Trim the areas marked "C" with a slanted cut to elevate the body. Trim the areas marked "D" to elevate the fin of the seahorse.

STEP 3

Trim away the area marked "A" surrounding the seahorse and seaweeds with a slanting cut approximately two inches long and one inch deep, creating a V-shape that exposes the red inner portion of the watermelon. Use the tip of the paring knife to carve the rugged body of the seahorse and the seaweeds.

Apple Birds

Step 1

Follow the line marked "A" to cut one-half inch from the bottom of the apple. Save this for the tail. Follow the "B" lines, making two cuts approximately one inch deep and meeting as shown in the illustration. Leave a one-inch wide area in the middle of the top of the apple.

Step 2

With the wedge you removed from the apple, perform the same process you followed in Step 1, making the cuts only one-eighth inch deep. Perform the same cuts on the remaining portion of the apple, making three or four cuts for attaching the wings. Attach the wings and tail with a toothpick.

Step 3

To make the bird's head, cut away both sides of another apple, leaving a one-inch wide area in the middle where the stem is. Following the dotted lines on illustration, cut away as marked. Carve a hole, and insert an apple seed for the eye on each side. Attach the head to the body with a toothpick.

Underwater Reef Fish

STEP 1

Select a parsnip and trim it. Cut a slice from the center of the parsnip approximately one-and-one-half-inches thick. Trim the edge of both sides, shaping it into a convex disk. Cut away the shaded areas. Trim the area marked "A", slanting both sides in, leaving a quarter-inch thick area on the end of the tail.

STEP 2

Trim the area marked "A", slanting both sides and leaving the fins approximately a quarter-inch thick on the top and one-half-inch thick on the bottom. On the area marked "B", follow the arrows to trim both sides, slanting in to the mouth, displaying the side fins.

STEP 3

Following the dotted lines on the illustration, trim these areas on both sides, slightly rounding the body. Use the tip of a paring knife to carve the fine, detailed lines. Create the eyes by making a cavity with the tip of a paring knife and filling it with whole black pepper.

Pineapple Rooster

STEP 1

Trim the bottom end of a pineapple at a slant. Cut an area two inches thick on both sides, leaving the bottom uncut to serve as the wings. Push the wings back slightly, separating them from the body. Pierce them with a bamboo skewer to steady the rooster. Cut another half-inch slice from the pineapple for the base.

STEP 2

Cut off the top from another pineapple. Remove some of the leaves and trim the end slightly, forming a conical section as shown. Remove some leaves from the middle. Cut a hole on both sides and insert whole black pepper for the eyes.

STEP 3

Create the crown from a red pepper or carrot. Using a two-inch long, half-inch diameter carrot, trim one end in a horn shape. Carve a slot on both sides, and attach the head to the body with a bamboo skewer.

Onion Flower Basket

STEP 1

Cut a three-and-one-half-inch long piece of onion leek stem. Use the tip of the knife to pierce the stem one-half inch deep and slice it lengthwise. Make as many slices as you can. Spread the flower. To dye it, put the appropriate food coloring in cold water and soak the flower for 15 minutes. Drain.

STEP 2

Slice the onion leek leaf lengthwise in quarter-inch strips. Separate both sides, slanting them in the middle as shown by the arrows. Make the same slices, following the solid lines to separate the strips. Soak the leaf in cold water for 15 minutes.

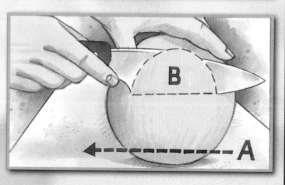

STEP 3

Make the cut shown by the "A" arrow, approximately one-half inch from the bottom, flattening the bottom of the honeydew melon basket. Make the cut shown by the "B" lines, cutting out both sides, leaving a two-inch-thick serving handle in the middle. Remove the seeds and assemble the flowers.

Carnival Village

THE PALM TREE

Starting at the top of a green bell pepper, make a V-shaped cut approximately two inches long, displaying the seeds. Attach a peeled carrot approximately seven inches long to the top of the pepper with a toothpick.

THE RADISH AND ZUCCHINI FLOWER

Make five slanted cuts on a red radish, cutting a small portion on both sides of the petals. Do the same on a zucchini, meeting all cuts in the middle to separate the flower as shown.

THE ZUCCHINI LEAF

On a whole zucchini, make slanted, convex cuts approximately five inches long and one-half inch thick in the middle portion. To carve the veins of the leaf, use the whole blade of the paring knife to make a long, V-shaped, shallow cut.

Carrot Flower Bouquet

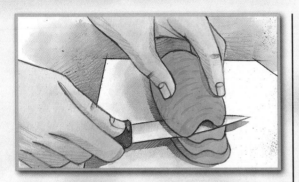

Step 1

Select a large, peeled carrot. Slightly round both ends, and cut a three-and-one-half-inch slice into the top. Cut slanted slices partially down the side of the carrot, stopping at the middle. (Make these slices as thin as possible.) Turn the carrot over and do the same on the other side so that the slices meet to create the first petal.

Step 2

Trim both sides of the carrot lengthwise, rounding it slightly. Repeat the same process as you used to make the first petal, trimming both sides until you create at least five petals. (The number of petals you will need depends on the size of the carrot.)

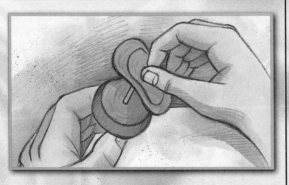

Step 3

Round the corners of the remaining portion of the carrot. Carve crossing lines for the buds of the flowers. Slice a quarter-inch-thick carrot, and pierce it in the middle with a bamboo skewer. Finally, pierce all the petals in alternate positions.

Ice Carving

Carnival's spectacular ice sculptures can add dramatic fire to any buffet spread.

Dolphins

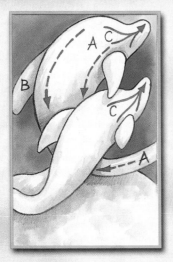   

STEP 1

Working from the back of the ice block, cut away the shaded areas. Trim the areas marked "A", slanting in approximately five inches to display the lower dolphin. Trim the areas marked "B" on both sides, leaving an area three inches thick for the back fins. Trim the areas marked "C", making sure the mouth is slightly pointed and the fins point out.

STEP 2

Trim the areas marked "A" approximately four inches deep to shape the tail of the lower dolphin. Trim the area marked "B" to separate the side fins of the upper dolphin. Trim the "C" area in the same way to separate the side fins of the lower dolphin. Trim the areas marked "D" to shape the tail of the upper dolphin.

STEP 3

Cut along the dotted lines to trim the edges, slightly rounding the bodies of both dolphins. Make slanting cuts approximately two inches deep in the areas indicated by the arrows to create waves on the base of the sculpture.

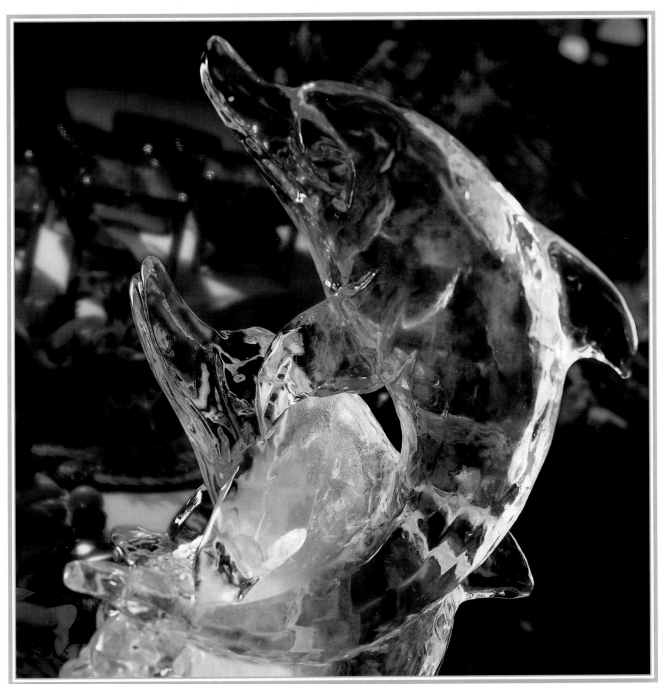

Love Birds

STEP 1

Working from the back of the ice block, cut out the shaded areas. Trim the areas marked "A" from the top of the head slanting down, so that the heads are approximately four-and-one-half inches thick. Trim the areas marked "B" approximately three inches deep, slanting into the body. Cut out the areas marked "C" approximately four inches deep.

STEP 2

Cut out the area marked "A" to separate the tip of the wings. Cut out the area marked "B", slanting in slightly to separate the base of the wings. Trim away the areas marked "C", shaping the tail but leaving the heart untouched. Trim and slightly round all edges of the body and head. Both sides of the carving should appear identical.

STEP 3

Trim the area marked "A" on both sides to shape the bill. Following the arrows along the wing, cut rows of feathers approximately three inches deep. Use a V-shaped chisel to carve the fine detail lines, and a C-shaped chisel to carve the fine feathers.

Lake Swans

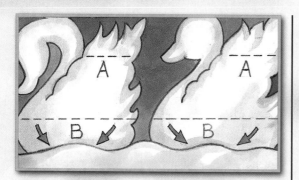

STEP 1

Working from the back of the ice block, cut away the shaded areas. Trim away the areas marked "A", slanting out and leaving tips of the wings six inches thick. Trim the areas marked "B" approximately four inches deep, slanting in and rounding slightly toward the base. Both sides of the swan should appear identical.

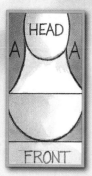

STEP 2

Cut away the shaded areas marked "A", shaping the neck and leaving the body untouched. Trim away the areas marked "B", slanting toward the neck to create the bill. Trim away the areas marked "C", slanting out toward the middle of the body. Trim away the area marked "D", slanting in toward the body approximately six inches deep.

STEP 3

Cut along the arrows approximately three inches deep, slanting in to create the waves at the base of the swans. Use a V-shaped chisel to carve the detailed lines, and a C-shaped chisel to carve the fine feathers.

Marlin Fish and Anchor

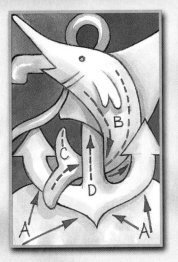
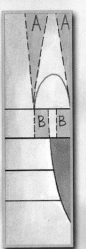

STEP 1

From the back of the ice block, cut away the shaded areas. Trim the areas marked "A" to slant in under the anchor approximately five inches deep. Trim the areas of the dotted line in the "B" section to slant in approximately five inches. Trim the areas marked "C" and "D" in the same way as you did the "A" sections.

STEP 2

Cut the "A" areas along the dotted lines to shape the head. Trim the "B" section into the body, shaping the lower fin. Trim the "C" section in the same method as "B" to shape the upper fin. Trim both blackened areas to shape the lower half of the tail.

STEP 3

Following the dotted lines, trim the areas to shape the whole body of the fish, slightly rounding it. Use a V-shaped chisel to carve the fine detail lines.

Carnival Buffets

Welcome to the secrets of the Carnival kitchens,
where every day we create magic to delight
both the eye and the palate.

Outdoor Buffet

The magic Carnival kitchens meet the great
outdoors, with recipes perfect for any
picnic, barbecue or elegant
backyard reception.

Gala Buffet

Enter a world of drama and elegance, with the pièce de résistance of the Carnival dining experience.

The tradition of cruising is one of elegance. Throughout this century, an ocean-going voyage has always meant adventure and prestige, and with that, the luxury of being treated virtually like royalty. That means elegance in accommodations, in entertainment, and most importantly, in fine dining. As we developed the "Fun Ship®" concept, Carnival recognized that retaining that sense of elegance was essential. And nothing maintains that grand tradition in grander style than the *pièce de résistance* of the Carnival experience, the Gala Buffet.

Traditionally the highlight of a Carnival cruise, the Gala Buffet marks the culmination of over 70 hours of work by 50 to 60 chefs and assistants, each drawing from the culinary traditions of his own country. This wealth of talent and heritage is blended in a creative mélange that results in a grand display of foods and desserts beyond most guests' wildest imagination.

Every element is carefully arranged to ensure that the buffet is an intriguing dining experience. The food is traditionally served at the stroke of midnight on the Captain's Gala Evening. The unveiling of the buffet table is always anxiously anticipated, especially by repeat cruise guests who have experienced the magic of other Gala Buffets in the past.

A Feast for the Eyes

For first-time guests, virtually nothing can prepare them for what they see at the stroke of twelve – the stuff of fantasy, a feast for both the eyes and the palate. Dish after dish, each more magnificent than the last. Carved and decorated hams, turkeys, chickens, terrines, and lobster. The extravagant "Flock of Birds," made completely of colorful, fresh vegetables. The dolphin ice sculpture and the seahorse formed from watermelon. And the "Green Dragon of Fire" carved entirely by hand from four blocks of solid ice, each weighing over 300 pounds!

Because of the pride they take in their work, the Carnival chefs continually attempt to outdo their last masterpiece, making the next Gala Buffet the most fantastic ever. That means inventing remarkable new temptations for the taste buds, and then challenging themselves to make the buffet presentation as breath-taking as the food is satisfying. That's why many regular Carnival guests tell us the Gala Buffet becomes more and more impressive every year.

It is estimated that Carnival guests take over 6,000 photographs of the stunning Gala Buffet every week. It has ensconced itself as part of the American tradition. In almost every town, someone, somewhere will treasure that special memento – a photo of their first Carnival Gala Buffet.

Of course, the exclamations of awe and wonder at the Carnival Gala Buffets are often followed by questions about the secrets of the Carnival kitchens. Can these masterpieces be created at home? This book is designed to give you some insight into the foods and designs that make up our Gala Buffets.

Even if your idea of cooking rarely tends to creations this elaborate, the photos and descriptions found here can bring back fond memories of the colors, tastes and smells that accompanied the unique Gala Buffet served on one of your cruises. For those of you who are more adventuresome in the culinary arts, we hope this book helps you to recreate some of that Carnival magic for your family and friends.

Dessert Buffet

*The most sinful temptations from the Carnival
kitchens, combining the richest creams,
the smoothest sauces, and, of course,
the finest chocolate.*

Buffet International

*Bring together the most succulent flavors of
France, Italy, Sweden, Japan
— all on one table.*

Volume Recipes

Take a peek into the Carnival kitchens, where
you can see how our chefs create rich
and exotic flavors for thousands.

Romaine Lettuce with Warm Brie Dressing

SERVES 100

This warm, garlicky dressing combines one of the world's great cheeses with lemon and Dijon mustard.

olive oil	2 qt
shallots, finely chopped	3 lb
finely chopped garlic	1½ cups
Brie cheese, chopped	8 lb
sherry vinegar	4 cups
lemon juice	2 cups
Dijon mustard	1 cup
salt	to taste
black pepper	to taste
romaine lettuce	12 heads

In large saucepan, heat olive oil. Add shallots and garlic; cook and stir until translucent. Add cheese, vinegar, lemon juice and mustard; blend well. Cook and stir over low heat until thickened and smooth. If necessary, add additional vinegar until dressing is of coating consistency. Season with salt and pepper.

Cut and wash lettuce; drain. Toss lettuce with warm dressing.

Pictured at right: one of our many wonderful appetizers. Although served in volume, each and every dish our chefs create is a work of art.

West Indian Pumpkin Soup

SERVES 100

A rich, creamy soup provides a savory new way to
bring out the classic pumpkin flavor.

onions, quartered	3 lb
leeks	2 lb
garlic cloves	2 oz
olive oil	2 fl oz
pumpkin puree	7 lb
chicken stock*	3½ gal
half-and-half	2 qt
heavy cream	1 qt
salt	to taste
black pepper	to taste

Heat oven to 300°F. Place onions, leeks and garlic in shallow roasting pan; drizzle with olive oil. Bake at 300°F. for 30 minutes. Puree vegetables.

Roast pumpkin puree at 300°F. for 20 to 25 minutes. In large stockpot, combine pumpkin puree, pureed vegetables and chicken stock; bring to a boil. Simmer 1 hour.

Add half-and-half and cream; simmer 5 minutes. Season with salt and pepper.

*See Chicken Stock recipe, p. 84.

Grilled Quail over Saffron Polenta

SERVES 100

*The taste of quail is graced with an exotic mixture of cherries
and mustard, and served with a hearty Italian polenta.*

CHERRY-MUSTARD SAUCE

Bing cherries, pitted	3 lb
cranberry sauce	1 lb
honey	1 lb
dry mustard	4 oz
horseradish	3 oz
glace de poulet*	1 gal
salt	to taste
black pepper	to taste

QUAIL

quail	100
salt	to taste
black pepper	to taste

POLENTA

chicken stock*	2 qt
butter	2 cups
saffron	¼ oz
salt	to taste
white pepper	to taste
cornmeal (polenta)	5 lb

In food processor, puree half of cherries with cranberry sauce, honey, mustard, horseradish and glace de poulet; place in large saucepan. Add remaining cherries; simmer 30 to 45 minutes. Season with salt and pepper.

Heat oven to 300°F. Remove backbone and separate breasts and legs from each quail. Season quail with salt and pepper. Tie quail; place in shallow roasting pan. Brush with cherry-mustard sauce. Bake at 300°F. for 12 to 15 minutes or until juices run clear. Remove breast bones.

Meanwhile, in large stockpot, combine chicken stock, butter, saffron, salt and white pepper; bring to a boil. Add cornmeal; boil 10 to 15 minutes or until cooked. Serve quail on bed of polenta; drizzle cherry-mustard sauce over top.

**See Glace de Poulet recipe, p. 84.
Chicken Stock recipe, p. 84.*

Pecan Pie

SERVES 96; 12 (10-INCH) PIES

With this recipe, the flavors of classic Southern pecan pie
can feed the largest gatherings.

brown sugar	3¼ **lb**
salt	¼ **oz**
dark corn syrup	3½ **lb**
butter, melted	14 **oz**
dark rum	3 **cups**
water	1 **tbsp**
vanilla	¼ **fl oz**
whole eggs	3½ **lb**
durum wheat flour	1¼ **oz**
chopped pecans	2½ **lb**
baked pie shells (10-inch)	12
apricot glaze	2 **lb**

Heat oven to 350°F. In large saucepan, combine brown sugar, salt, corn syrup, melted butter, rum, water and vanilla; mix well. Simmer until mixture reaches 120°F. Strain; set aside.

In large bowl, whisk eggs until beaten. Add flour; whip until blended. Add to syrup mixture; blend well. Strain.

Divide pecans evenly into pie shells. Pour syrup mixture evenly into shells over pecans.

Bake at 350°F. for 25 to 30 minutes or until filling is completely set. Brush each pie with boiled apricot glaze. Cut each pie into 8 pieces.

Recipes for Entertaining

Carnival chefs show you the secrets of a table that will impress and delight your guests.

New England Style Boiled Lobster

SERVES 6

This traditional entree from the Eastern Seaboard enhances the succulent
flavors of steamed lobster with lemon and melted butter.

rib of celery	1
leek	1
carrot	1
butter	2 tbsp
sea salt	to taste
Maine lobsters (16 to 20 oz. each)	6
lemons, cut into thin slices	2
melted butter	5 tbsp

Clean and peel celery, leek and carrot; cut into 2-inch-long strips. In large skillet, cook vegetables in butter until crisp-tender. Season with salt.

Bring salted water to a boil. Add live lobsters; reduce heat and simmer about 6 minutes. Remove lobsters from water. Cut into halves; break claws open. Place lobsters on serving plates. Garnish with vegetables and lemon twists. Serve with melted butter.

Scampi Marinati alla Griglia

SERVES 6

This tomato-based shrimp entree includes pasta created with the exotic flavors of spinach, beet root and squid ink.

PASTA

durum wheat flour	1½ lb
salt	1 tsp
eggs	6
semolina	6 oz
spinach puree	½ cup
beet root puree	½ cup
squid ink	1 tsp

SHRIMP

shelled deveined jumbo shrimp	2 lb
fresh lemon juice	2 tbsp
minced garlic	1 tsp
salt	to taste
extra-virgin olive oil	½ cup
butter	1 cup
chopped shallots	½ cup
minced garlic	½ tsp
white wine	½ cup
tomato concasse*	1½ cups
chopped fresh Italian parsley	¼ cup

In large bowl, combine flour, salt and eggs; mix well. On semolina-dusted surface, knead dough until smooth. Divide dough into 3 equal portions. Add spinach puree, beet root puree and squid ink to respective portions; mix each well. Cover dough; let rest 30 minutes.

Meanwhile, marinate shrimp in lemon juice, 1 teaspoon garlic and salt for 30 minutes.

With pasta rolling machine, pass dough through linguine cutter. Boil pasta in salted boiling water for 5 to 7 minutes or until al dente.

In large heavy skillet, heat oil over high heat until hot. Add shrimp; cook and toss quickly for about 2 minutes. Remove shrimp from skillet; set aside.

In same skillet, melt half of butter. Add shallots; cook until soft. Add garlic and pan juices from shrimp. Add wine; cook, stirring to loosen browned bits from bottom of skillet. Add tomato concasse and remaining half of butter; cook until sauce thickens. Sprinkle with parsley. Serve pasta with shrimp and sauce.

*See Tomato Concasse recipe, p. 84.

Smoked Chicken Quesadillas

SERVES 6

A flour tortilla is filled with savory smoked chicken and a variety of spicy Mexican flavors.
It can be served as an entree or cut into wedges to be eaten as an appetizer.

boneless skinless chicken breasts	**1 lb**
chopped garlic	**1 tbsp**
liquid smoke	**½ tsp**
chopped onion	**½ cup**
finely diced carrot	**½ cup**
finely diced celery	**¼ cup**
jalapeño chile	**1**
fajita seasoning	**2 tbsp**
cumin	**1 tsp**
fresh lemon juice	**1 tsp**
salt	**to taste**
black pepper	**to taste**
chopped green onion tops	**½ cup**
chopped fresh cilantro	**¼ cup**
shredded Monterey Jack cheese	**½ cup**
flour tortillas (8-inch)	**6**
sour cream	**1 cup**
guacamole	**1 cup**

Marinate chicken in garlic and liquid smoke for 4 to 5 hours.

Grill chicken, or in large skillet, cook chicken a few minutes on each side or until juices run clear. Dice chicken. In same skillet, cook onion, carrot, celery and chile for a few minutes. Stir in chicken. Add fajita seasoning, cumin, lemon juice, salt and pepper; cook until thoroughly heated. Add green onions, cilantro and cheese.

Heat tortillas on warm flat-top grill at 250°F. Place chicken mixture on one side of each tortilla; fold remaining half of tortilla over mixture. Grill quesadillas on each side. Serve with sour cream and guacamole.

Eggplant Napoleon

SERVES 6

The classic layering techniques of a Napoleon-style dessert prepared in a fresh, new way, combining cheese, mushrooms, eggplant and olives.

red bell peppers	2
large eggplants	2
fresh mushrooms	1½ lb
olive oil	½ cup
chopped fresh oregano	2 tbsp
chopped fresh thyme	2 tbsp
garlic cloves, crushed	4
sliced mozzarella cheese	12 oz
sliced pitted black olives	1 cup
finely diced yellow onions	1 cup
tomato sauce	1 cup

Heat oven to 300°F. Roast bell peppers in oven for 10 to 12 minutes. Cool peppers. Remove and discard seeds; dice peppers. Slice eggplants into ¼-inch-thick slices. Slice mushrooms.

In small bowl, combine oil, oregano, thyme and garlic; blend well. Lightly brush eggplant slices with oil mixture. In large skillet, cook eggplant over high heat for 30 seconds on each side. Remove eggplant from skillet; set aside. Cook mushrooms in skillet with a small amount of oil mixture until tender. Remove mushrooms from skillet; set aside.

In large baking pan, layer half of eggplant, half of cheese, olives, onions, bell peppers and mushrooms. Top with remaining eggplant and cheese.

Bake at 300°F. for 20 minutes. Serve with tomato sauce.

Shrimp Salad

Pictured on page 67

SERVES 8

Light yet satisfying, and can be served as a meal starter or by itself.

shrimp titi	½ **lb**
mayonnaise	½ **cup**
finely chopped onion	¼ **cup**
finely chopped celery	¼ **cup**
chopped fresh parsley	**pinch**
salt	**to taste**
white pepper	**to taste**

Drain shrimp of excess water. In large bowl, whisk mayonnaise until smooth. Add onion, celery, parsley, salt and pepper; mix well. Fold in shrimp. To serve, arrange lettuce on bread slices; top with shrimp salad.

Pickled Herring

Pictured on page 67

SERVES 6

*A taste from the northern shores of Scandinavia, this excellent appetizer or garnish
adds the unique zest of ginger and an array of colorful pickled vegetables.*

boneless small herring fillets (skin on)	**12**
sea salt (coarse)	**3 tbsp**
sliced celery	**2 oz**
sliced red onion	**2 oz**
sliced carrots	**2 oz**
sliced peeled parsnips	**2 oz**
grated fresh ginger	**2 oz**
white wine vinegar	**2 cups**
water	**½ cup**
mustard seeds	**1 tbsp**
sugar	**2 tsp**
garlic cloves, peeled	**3**
sprigs fresh coriander or cilantro	**3**
sprigs fresh Italian parsley	**3**
bay leaves	**2**

Rub herring fillets generously with sea salt; arrange in shallow dish. Cover; refrigerate about 12 hours to marinate.

In large saucepan, combine all remaining ingredients. Bring to a boil. Boil 1 minute. Remove from heat; cool.

Remove excess salt from fish. Pour vinegar mixture over fish in dish. Cover; refrigerate 3 to 4 days.

Gravlax

Pictured on page 67

SERVES 6

Prized around the world, this Swedish specialty features raw salmon cured in a mixture of salt, sugar and dill.

boneless salmon fillets (skin on, scales removed)	**2 lb**
white peppercorns	**1 tsp**
black peppercorns	**1 tsp**
coriander seeds	**1 tsp**
mustard seeds	**1 tsp**
sugar	**3 oz**
sea salt (coarse)	**2 oz**
coarsely chopped fresh dill	**½ cup**

Dry fillets with paper towels. Separately roast peppercorns, coriander seeds and mustard seeds. Pound all peppercorns and all seeds with sugar and salt to make a coarse marinade.

Sprinkle marinade and half of the chopped dill liberally over flesh side of salmon fillets. Sprinkle some of the marinade on skin side of salmon; place in stainless steel pan. Cover tightly with plastic wrap; place weight on wrap over salmon to keep it weighed down. Refrigerate 48 hours on each side.

Drain juices from salmon. Cut salmon into very thin slices.

Paella Valencia

SERVES 6

A Spanish dish of saffron-flavored rice with a variety of meats and shellfish,
it is named after the special two-handled pan — the paella
— in which it's traditionally prepared and served.

olive oil	½ cup
small chicken drumsticks	6
diced lean pork	8 oz
diced onions	4 oz
garlic cloves	¼ cup
diced green and red bell peppers	8 oz
diced leek	1 tsp
uncooked rice	1 lb
chicken stock*	1 qt
white wine	½ cup
salt	to taste
white pepper	to taste
saffron	pinch
shelled deveined large shrimp	6
chorizo	8 oz
8-oz lobster tails, cut in half	3
scallops	8 oz
mussels in shell or half shell	6
tomatoes, peeled, diced	1 lb
green peas	6 oz

Heat oil in large skillet. Add chicken drumsticks and pork; cook 15 to 20 minutes. Add onions, garlic, bell peppers and leeks; cook 2 minutes. Set aside. Add rice with small amount of oil to same skillet; cook and stir.

Add chicken stock, wine, salt, pepper and saffron; bring to a boil. Cook until rice is half done.

Return chicken, pork and vegetables to skillet; add shrimp, chorizo and lobster. Just before rice is ready, add scallops, mussels, tomatoes and peas.

*See Chicken Stock recipe, p. 84.

Roast Crown of Veal

SERVES 6

*Fit for a king, this beautifully presented entree is formed from the rib section of veal,
tied into a circle, ribs up, with the hollow center section
filled with mixed vegetables.*

veal rack (6 ribs)	4 lb
olive oil	2 fl oz
sea salt (coarse)	2 oz
crushed black pepper	1 oz
sprigs fresh rosemary	3
sprigs fresh thyme	3
veal stock	2 qt
Yukon gold potatoes	1 lb
baby carrots	6
baby turnips	6
golden beets	6
shallots	6
butter, melted	8 oz

Heat oven to 450°F. Trim excess fat from veal rack; clean bones at least 2 inches down from top. Season veal with olive oil, salt, pepper, rosemary and thyme. Shape veal rack into round shape, inside out, tying with butcher twine; place in shallow roasting pan.

Bake at 450°F. for 10 minutes. Reduce oven temperature to 350°F.; bake an additional 40 minutes for "medium well" or to desired doneness. Baste veal occasionally with veal stock during baking.

Remove veal from pan; cover to keep warm. Place pan over medium heat; pour remaining veal stock into pan. Cook, stirring to loosen browned bits from bottom of pan; simmer until stock becomes a sauce. Strain; season to taste.

Clean and peel vegetables. In large saucepan, simmer vegetables in salted water until crisp-tender. Drain; return to saucepan. Toss with melted butter.

Place veal rack on serving tray; arrange vegetables in center of rack and around tray. Sprinkle veal with a small amount of sauce; serve remaining sauce on the side.

Honey-Glazed Baby Back Ribs

Pictured on page 75

SERVES 6

*Sweet but spicy, this glaze is a hearty and unusual treat
for rib lovers used to more traditional sauces.*

barbecue sauce	1 cup
honey	½ cup
onions, quartered	2
garlic cloves	10
whole cloves	8
bay leaves	3
cinnamon stick	1
dried thyme leaves	1 tsp
black peppercorns	1 tsp
crushed red pepper flakes	1 tsp
pork baby back ribs	4 lb

In medium bowl, combine barbecue sauce and honey; mix well. Set aside.

In large stockpot, combine 3 gallons of water with all remaining ingredients except ribs. Bring to a boil. Add ribs; simmer 20 to 30 minutes, skimming surface occasionally to remove foam.

Heat oven to 300°F. Remove cooked ribs from stockpot; place in shallow roasting pan. Brush generously with sauce mixture. Bake at 300°F. for 25 to 30 minutes or until very tender and meat can be removed easily from bones.

Blackened Sirloin with Grilled Corn on the Cob

Pictured on page 75

SERVES 6

Traditional steak and corn on the cob get a dramatic new twist with cayenne pepper and Cajun cooking techniques.

CORN

oil	¼ cup
garlic clove, minced	1
chopped fresh oregano	1 tsp
chopped fresh thyme	1 tsp
ears corn on the cob	6

SIRLOIN

beef sirloin strip steaks	6
black pepper	3 tsp
dried oregano leaves	2 tsp
dried thyme leaves	2 tsp
salt	1 tsp
cayenne pepper	½ tsp

Heat grill to 300°F. In small bowl, combine oil, garlic, oregano and thyme; mix well. Remove husks from corn. Brush corn generously with oil mixture. Grill corn at 300°F. for 10 to 15 minutes or until tender.

Meanwhile, with cloth towel, remove excess moisture from each steak. In small bowl, combine all remaining sirloin ingredients. Sprinkle steaks generously with mixture. Brush grill with oil; grill steaks at 300°F. for 4 to 5 minutes on each side or until desired doneness. Serve corn with steaks.

Corn Bread

Pictured on page 75

SERVES 6

*Best when served hot from the oven, corn bread is the perfect complement for
dozens of entrées, from early-morning breakfasts to late-night suppers.*

cornmeal	1 cup
all-purpose flour	½ cup
baking powder	1 tsp
salt	½ tsp
egg yolks	2
water	2 cups
butter, softened	2 tbsp
maple syrup	2 tsp
egg whites	3
sugar	2 tbsp

Heat oven to 375°F. Line 8-inch mold with parchment paper. In large bowl, combine cornmeal, flour, baking powder and salt; mix well. In small bowl, whisk yolks, water, butter and maple syrup until smooth. Pour into cornmeal mixture; mix until free of lumps.

In another small bowl, whisk egg whites with sugar until peaks form. Fold into batter. Pour into prepared mold. Bake at 375°F. for 20 to 30 minutes or until top springs back when touched lightly in center.

California Roll

Pictured on page 78

SERVES 6

Inspired by the sunny flavors of California, this version of sushi incorporates flavorful avocado with crab meat and sushi rice.

avocado	1
cream cheese	2 oz
crabmeat	2 oz
soy sauce	1 tsp
nori sheets (dried seaweed)	2
sushi rice*	2 cups
rice wine vinegar	1 tsp
wasabi (Japanese horseradish)	dash

Peel and pit avocado. Cut avocado and cream cheese into ½-inch strips. Season crabmeat with soy sauce.

Place 1 nori sheet, glossy side down, on sushi mat. Spread 1 cup rice evenly over sheet with the help of rice vinegar. Sprinkle with dash wasabi (very hot). Place half of crabmeat lengthwise over rice; top with half of avocado and cream cheese. Roll up tightly with the help of sushi mat. Slice roll into 6 pieces. Repeat with second nori sheet.

See Sushi Rice recipe, p. 81.

Sushi with Salmon Roe

Pictured on page 78

SERVES 6

This sushi features the exotic taste of salmon caviar, a simple way to add an elegant touch to hors d'oeuvres.

sushi rice*	1 cup
wasabi (Japanese horseradish)	dash
nori sheets (dried seaweed)	2
salmon roe	6 oz

Divide rice into 12 equal portions. Apply a little wasabi to palms of hands; shape rice into balls. Press each to form a round.

Cut each nori sheet into 6 equal strips as marked on the sheets. With rice round at base of strip, wrap nori strip around rice. Fill each with salmon roe.

**See Sushi Rice recipe, p. 81.*

Sushi with Salmon

Pictured on page 78

SERVES 6

For salmon lovers, this sushi is a traditional Japanese approach to bring out new depths of flavor.

nori sheet (dried seaweed)	1
sushi rice*	2 cups
rice wine vinegar	½ cup
salmon fillet (sashimi grade)	6 oz
wasabi (Japanese horseradish)	dash

Cut nori sheet into 12 equal ribbons. Set aside.

Divide rice into 12 equal portions. With help of vinegar and water, shape each portion into an oval.

Cut salmon into strips, 1½ inches long and ¾ inch wide. Apply small amount of wasabi to each strip of salmon. Cover each oval of rice with salmon, making sure rice is completely covered. Wrap a ribbon of nori around center of each salmon sushi.

**See Sushi Rice recipe, p. 81.*

Sushi with Tuna

Pictured on page 78

SERVES 6

*One of the most popular types of sushi, it is simple
to prepare and full of fresh tuna flavor.*

sushi rice*	2 cups
rice wine vinegar	½ cup
tuna (sashimi grade)	6 oz
wasabi (Japanese horseradish)	dash

Divide rice into 12 equal portions. With help of vinegar and water, shape each portion into an oval.

Cut tuna into slices, 1½ inches long and ¾ inch wide. Apply small amount of wasabi to each slice of tuna. Cover each oval of rice with tuna, making sure rice is completely covered.

*See Sushi Rice recipe, below.

Sushi Rice

YIELD 3 CUPS

*Sushi rice has a sticky consistency when cooked,
making it ideal for sushi.*

uncooked Japanese sushi rice	1½ cups
water	3 cups
rice vinegar	5 tbsp
sugar	2 tsp
salt	to taste

Rinse rice with cold water. In medium saucepan, combine rice and water. Bring to a boil. Reduce heat; cook until rice has absorbed all water. Remove from heat; set aside for 2 to 3 hours to cool.

In small bowl, combine vinegar, sugar and salt; mix well. Place cooled, cooked rice in large bowl. Add vinegar mixture; stir until rice is free of lumps and well coated.

Chocolate Gateau

SERVES 12

*Rich and chocolatey, with succulent strawberries
and a sinful touch of chocolate liqueur.*

melted white chocolate	1 cup
chocolate sponge cake*	1 recipe
chocolate liqueur	1 tbsp
apricot glaze	¼ cup
chocolate buttercream*	½ cup
chocolate ganache*	1 recipe
melted sweet chocolate	¼ cup
fresh strawberries	12

Place melted white chocolate in paper bag; cut off corner of bag so a thick layer of chocolate can be piped. Pipe an "S", not to exceed 3 inches long and ¼ inch wide, on parchment paper. Repeat until all chocolate is used. Refrigerate.

Cut sponge cake horizontally into 3 layers. Place first cake layer on serving tray; sprinkle with liqueur. Spread with glaze and chocolate buttercream. Repeat with second layer. Place third cake layer on top of cake. Spread entire cake with chocolate buttercream. Refrigerate 30 minutes.

Spread ganache evenly on surface of cake. Pipe 12 rosettes of buttercream onto cake.

Using another paper bag filled with melted sweet chocolate and corner cut off, make cross-lines of chocolate on outside of cake. Remove "S's" from paper; arrange on top of cake. Garnish with strawberries.

*See Chocolate Sponge Cake recipe, p. 85.
Chocolate Buttercream recipe, p. 85.
Chocolate Ganache recipe, p. 85.*

Tomato Concasse

YIELD 2 CUPS

chopped peeled shallots	2 oz
extra-virgin olive oil	1 oz
cubed, peeled, seeded tomatoes	2 cups
salt	to taste

In large skillet, cook shallots in olive oil for 3 to 4 minutes or until translucent. Add tomatoes; cook an additional 3 minutes. Season with salt.

Tip: Depending on use for tomato concasse, other ingredients such as garlic, pepper or fresh herbs may need to be added.

Chicken Stock

YIELD 1 GALLON

chicken necks	5 lb
water	5 gal
onions, coarsely chopped	1 lb
carrots, coarsely chopped	1 lb
leeks, coarsely chopped	1 lb
peppercorns	1 tsp
bay leaves	3
sprigs fresh thyme	2

Wash chicken necks; place in large saucepot. Add water; bring to a boil. Boil 5 minutes. Remove from heat. Strain, reserving stock. Discard bones. Return stock to saucepot.

Add vegetables, peppercorns, bay leaves and thyme. Bring to a boil over high heat. Skim surface to remove foam. Reduce heat to medium; simmer 3 to 4 hours. Remove from heat; strain.

Glace de Poulet

YIELD 1 CUP

chicken bones	1 lb
cold water	3 qt
white wine	1 cup
chopped onions	1½ cups
chopped carrot	1 cup
chopped leek	¼ cup
white peppercorns	1 tbsp
bay leaf	1
salt	to taste
white pepper	to taste

In 4-quart saucepan, combine chicken bones and water. Bring to a boil over high heat. Simmer 5 minutes. Add all remaining ingredients; cook until mixture comes to a boil. Reduce heat to low; simmer 1 to 2 hours. Skim surface occasionally to remove foam.

Remove from heat; strain. Return stock to saucepan. Bring to a boil over high heat. Cook until reduced by three-fourths. Season to taste with salt and pepper.

Chocolate Sponge Cake

SERVES 6

sugar	½ cup
vanilla	¼ tsp
eggs	4
sifted cake flour	1¼ cups
unsweetened cocoa	2 tbsp

Heat oven to 375°F. Grease and flour 6-inch round cake pan. In medium bowl, combine sugar, vanilla and eggs. Place bowl over warm water; whisk constantly until mixture reaches 110°F. (Sugar will be completely dissolved.) Remove bowl from water bath. Continue whisking until very light and fluffy.

Sift flour and cocoa together. Fold into egg mixture. Pour into greased and floured pan.

Bake at 375°F. for 25 minutes or until cake springs back when touched lightly in center. Cool on wire rack. Cool completely before removing from pan.

Tip: A 6-inch round cake pan can be purchased at specialty stores with cake decorating supplies. If a larger pan is used, decrease bake time.

Chocolate Ganache

SERVES 6

semi-sweet chocolate, chopped	9 oz
hot whole milk	1 cup
butter, softened	1½ tsp

Place chocolate in small bowl. Place bowl over simmering water; stir chocolate until melted. Add hot milk; stir gently to mix. Add butter; remove bowl from simmering water. Continue stirring chocolate until completely cooled and smooth.

Tip: Be careful no water gets into chocolate or chocolate will seize (clump and harden).

Chocolate Buttercream

SERVES 6

sugar	½ cup
water	3½ tbsp
light corn syrup	1 tsp
eggs	2
salt	¼ tsp
butter, softened	1 cup
semi-sweet chocolate chips, melted, cooled	1 cup

In small saucepan, combine sugar, water and corn syrup; mix well. Bring to a boil over high heat; boil 1½ minutes.

In large bowl, beat eggs and salt at high speed until foamy. While beating at high speed, slowly pour hot syrup into eggs. Continue beating until mixture is light, fluffy and cooled. At medium speed, beat in butter; continue beating for 3 minutes. Add cooled melted chocolate; beat about 2 minutes or until light and fluffy.

Tip: Because of food safety, only pasteurized eggs should be used in recipes when the eggs are not cooked.

Index